Investing

An All Inclusive Guide To Stock Trading: Your Blueprint
For Successful Investing And Trading In The Stock
Market

*(Unlocking The Mysteries Of Investing For The Highest
Possible Returns)*

Dominique Kofler

TABLE OF CONTENT

How To Get Started Making Money With Dividend Stocks

Take the following steps once you are ready to begin investing in dividend stocks in order to achieve your objectives regarding the generation of passive income.

1. Pick out an existing account.

When getting started with dividend investing, the first thing you should think about is choosing the appropriate account. This is due to the fact that dividends are subject to taxation in certain nations, making it imperative to have accounts that are registered. If you do not have sufficient information about the many sorts of accounts that are accessible, you run the risk of becoming confused since you will not be able to comprehend how to choose the account that is most appropriate for your requirements.

2. Decide on a broker to work with.

You need to find a broker who provides the kind of account that you require for this investment, and you need to do this as soon as possible. You also need to decide as soon as possible whether or not you will use a dividend reinvestment plan (DRIP) with your investment and choose a broker who is familiar with this tactic.

3. Invest in either exchange-traded funds or stocks.

Only trading in individual equities is permitted on the vast majority of conventional investment platforms. However, a number of contemporary platforms have expanded their offerings to incorporate ETFs, which make it simpler for investors to diversify the holdings of their portfolio. A handful of exchange-traded funds that track indexes place an emphasis on accumulating dividend income while charging exceptionally minimal costs. When it comes to investing in dividend stocks, using exchange-traded funds (ETFs) can be beneficial because it eliminates the requirement that investors have a solid understanding of the underlying firms. Your primary concentration should be only on the total amount of money that will be returned to you in the form of passive income.

4. Increase the value of your assets.

The process of earning an income from dividend stocks does not finish with the purchase of stock. There are further steps involved. In order to increase the returns on your passive income investments, you will need to continue making consistent payments as well as reinvesting any dividends that you receive. Because of this, the growth of your profits will be accelerated.

Choosing the Appropriate Stock

There are a variety of measures that you can use to determine how lucrative an investment opportunity is, which can be helpful if you are trying to choose the correct stock to put your money into. The dividend yield is one example of this type of measure. As was said earlier, the dividend yield provides an estimate of the percentage of the stock price that will be distributed to shareholders in the form of dividends. The dividend yield directly correlates to the amount of income received. Another metric to look at is whether or not the company can keep up with its dividend payments. You may learn this information by analyzing the company's capacity to create a good profit, which is where the dividends will come from, therefore examining the company's potential profit will provide you this information. The extent to which the amount of the dividend has the potential to increase in the coming years is still another criterion. The higher your dividend increases, the more money you will earn in the form of passive income.

The greatest stock to invest in for dividends is one that has a track record of consistently paying out solid dividends. The majority of equities that have a stable history also have a good chance of having a stable future. Find those stocks that have a long-term investment horizon of at least ten years and invest in those. Consider investing in the stocks of businesses that are involved in the economies of more than one sector and more than one nation.

Needs in Terms of Cash

When you initially start investing in dividend stocks, the first thing you need to do is determine how much money you need each year in order to be able to achieve the goals you have set for your investments. It is easy to calculate how much capital you require to get started once you have determined how much revenue you require from the venture. If you plan to subsist solely off of this income, you may figure out how much money you need to bring in each month based on how much it currently costs you to maintain your standard of living.

In the following illustration, we will make the assumption that you require an annual income of $500,000.00 in order to lead a life of comfort and contentment. This indicates that you need a dividend stock portfolio of approximately one million dollars in it in order to be able to depend fully on passive income. When discussing the stock market, this does not mean that you are necessary to make all of these investments at once in order to achieve the desired level of income. The value of your investment in the stock market will increase by a predetermined amount each year. This indicates that if you invest half of this money over the course of approximately six years, you will finish up with one million dollars. If you choose to invest 10% of this, then it will take you 19 years to grow this amount to its current level.

How to Know When to Take Profit from an Investment

Over the course of time, a number of the exciting investment options that you initially considered are not going to pan out. If you have made smart choices, most of them will continue to be stable, and they will most likely provide good dividends. On the other hand, it is an inevitable part of life that some businesses will disappear from view at some point. It is possible that you will discover that the corporation is unable to continue paying dividends at the level that you were anticipating receiving. Or, the company's share price could plummet for one of a number of different reasons. It is possible that it will be driven out of a market or perhaps made to declare bankruptcy. Many businesses that were formerly stable have run into significant difficulties and some have even been forced to shut their doors. Consider the case of Lumber Liquidators, whose stock price plummeted to the point where it was worthless after the media reported on a controversy involving chemicals found in the company's wood flooring. Because

General Motors came so close to filing for bankruptcy, the value of the company's stock plummeted. Another illustration of this is the investment bank Bear-Sterns, which had a history dating back one hundred years and was widely regarded as a rock-solid investment. During the financial crisis that hit in 2008, the value of the corporation was completely wiped out as a result of the falling value of mortgage securities.

Consequently, there is no assurance that the money you invest today will still be there for you the next day. That is why having a diversified portfolio is essential. If you have a significantly diversified portfolio, losing everything on a single GM or Bear-Sterns investment is not likely to happen.

The ability to judge when to withdraw your money is crucial. To begin, you will need to ensure that you are paying attention to the news that pertains to a particular organization. It is in your best interest to sell your shares before the price of the company's stock begins a precipitous decline. This will allow you to not only recoup the money you initially placed into the stock but also to reinvest it in a different business that offers dividends.

If disastrous news about a firm in which you have invested reaches the media, this is probably a circumstance in which you are going to want to reassess your investments since it puts you in a position where you could lose all of your money. When doing your assessment of the circumstance, it is imperative that you make use of cautious and well-reasoned thinking. When terrible news about a company comes out, you shouldn't automatically freak out. It is not uncommon for unfavorable information to become public, but the effects it has on the organization are often temporary.

The majority of the time, when we discuss selling dividend-paying stocks, we are going to be thinking about a scenario in which the share price of the stock has been progressively decreasing over a lengthy period of time, and/or they are paying lower dividend payments. This is because both of these things tend to occur simultaneously. On a yearly basis, you should conduct an analysis to determine how well your investments are doing. Therefore, in addition to performing rebalancing at the start of each year, you should have a look at each of your individual assets to evaluate how well it has performed and to determine whether or not the stock continues to exhibit a healthy appearance.

If you begin to recognize issues, it may be time to sell your stock and look for another investment opportunity. You might have another stock that is doing considerably better than the one that is languishing or falling in value, and it might be a good idea to move your money into the new investment rather of staying in the stock that is doing poorly or falling in value.

It is important to keep in mind that you do not automatically have to sell a stock that appears to be going for trouble as soon as you notice the warning signs. You have the option of taking a strategy that involves progressively minimizing your exposure. As an illustration, you may move 25% of your investment away from the problematic stock and into either brand new assets or current investments that appear to be performing better. The situation should then be reassessed some time later, perhaps after a quarter has passed. Perhaps there will be an upturn in the company's performance in the near future. If it is still experiencing issues at that point, you have the option of withdrawing totally from the situation or continuing your progressive approach. You have the option of selling off another 25% of the investment and then waiting another quarter to see if the company has improved its financial situation; if it has, then you may wish to keep the investment in your portfolio.

You might have some firms in your portfolio that are performing okay, but they have not turned out to be that wonderful. On the other hand, you might come across a company that seems like a superior dividend investment. Both of these scenarios are possible. It's possible that this is the kind of scenario in which shifting your money from one investment to another might be the best course of action.

You are going to wish to take into consideration your fundamental analysis in each and every one of these scenarios. If a firm fails to meet expectations for a number of consecutive quarters, this can have a substantial negative impact on the stock price, which may be an indication that it is time to sell the stock. Keeping an eye on the dividend payout ratio could be of equal or greater significance. If a firm's earnings are falling behind its competitors but at the same time the company is paying out a large dividend to the point where the payout ratio goes over 100%, this may be an indication that the company is overvalued. It is not appropriate to respond to this matter with reflexive behaviors. When you realize that the payout ratio has increased, you do not want to immediately throw in the towel on the investment. Nevertheless, additional research is definitely required. You are going to want to give careful consideration to the basics of the organization, as well as its goals for the future. When conducting basic analysis, there are a number of factors that you need to take into consideration, and we will go over many of these factors in chapter 8.

Keep in mind that the fact that we only have access to incomplete information puts all of us at a disadvantage when it comes to making decisions regarding investments. The fact that we are unable to see into the future is one of the issues. Regarding the future, all we can do is make educated guesses and predictions.

Therefore, it is inevitable that there will be occasions when you get something wrong. It's possible that a business will give the impression of plunging headfirst into the muck, prompting you to consider selling off your investment. Then, after some time has passed, you may discover that the business has improved, at which point you may lament the decision to withdraw your investment. After that, you will start to fill your head with "what if?" scenarios, thinking about how much better off you would be if you had only stayed with the company instead of leaving it.

Investing, however, cannot be approached in this manner at all. You need to stop worrying about purported missed chances and instead center your attention on the successful aspects of your portfolio. Keep in mind that it will be preferable to prematurely get rid of an investment that appeared to be going bad, rather than to cling onto the investment for a great deal too long and end up losing a significant quantity of money as a result of doing so.

Why Am I Required To Pay Management Fees If The Etf Is A Passive Investment Option?

A few hundred years ago, in order to purchase ownership of a successful company, one required an army of lawyers, secretaries, offices, and most crucially, a significant amount of time. A little more than two hundred years ago, stock exchanges began to appear, which made it much easier to acquire ownership in a company. This facilitated greater economic activity.

The introduction of exchange-traded funds (ETFs) a little more than 20 years ago began the process of ETFs gradually replacing their financial ancestors, which made buying shares easier than driving a car. In today's market, it is possible to own ownership in almost any publicly traded firm, in almost any index you like!

Your ownership is not contingent on the guarantee of a particular investment property or any other property. The shares that you buy are actually purchased and deposited in a trust account with a third party. This account is held at a bank that is not affiliated with the investment company in which you invest. The number of shares that you owned on the day that the investment house filed for bankruptcy is the exact same number of shares that you continue to possess. As a result, your ownership will not be altered if the investment house files for bankruptcy.

How come it is priced so low?

Index funds can save you a significant amount of time and effort, cut the amount of money you have to pay in management fees, and save the amount of tax you have to pay on an ongoing basis. The management of a stock portfolio is not something that should be handled lightly, and it calls for a significant amount of research and focus.

When an investor wants to sell a share that has suddenly increased in value, they are required to pay a capital gains tax based on the amount that the share was sold for. On the occasion of this joyous occasion, the investment house will additionally levy a transaction fee, commonly known as purchase costs or sales fees. This "hunting" for stocks approach takes a lot of time and involves a significant financial investment from the investor. However, this is not the primary justification at all.

Reputation of the company that is granting the certificate - it's the same as completing a home inspection, except you can do it from the comfort of your own living room sofa.

Both Vanguard and BlackRock, better known as the iShares brand and both of which will be referenced quite a bit in this book as a result of their respective series of exchange-traded funds (ETFs), are considered to be the two most successful investing companies in the United States.

These two investment firms, along with many others like them, have been there for a significant amount of time, are subject to stringent regulation, and are responsible for an amount of money that is similar to the whole assets of numerous banks combined. This indicates that you may unquestionably rely on the success of any investments made through them.

On top of that, you might be astonished to learn that even in the event that the issuing firm goes bankrupt and liquidates its assets, those who invested via it will not be completely wiped out by the occurrence.

The lessons learned from history indicate that if an investment firm runs into financial difficulties, there is a good possibility that another investment firm will buy its assets and customers. Therefore, a situation of "catastrophic bankruptcy" is not at all common, and even if it does happen, there is a convincing safety net for investors who invested through it. In other words, there is a convincing safety net for investors. The assets, which, as was previously said, do not belong to the investment house but do belong to the investors, are held in trust rather than in the warehouse of the company. This indicates that in the event that the issuing firm declares bankruptcy, the profits from the sale of the securities will be distributed to the owners of those securities by the liquidator of the company, who will be a lawyer appointed by the court.

There is no valid cause to be concerned about the trustworthiness or longevity of huge investment institutions. Choosing to put your money into an organization that has a solid track record is the most successful strategy for trading exchange-traded funds (ETFs).

Ignore The Influence Of Other People.

Having the ability to control your emotions is a skill that must be developed over time and with effort. But it appears to be something that comes naturally to Buffett, despite the fact that he has been subjected to mockery on multiple occasions for failing to capitalize on significant market changes. One such example is the meteoric ascent of the technology and internet companies in the late 1990s and early 2000s. The Dow Jones industrial average increased by 25% in 1999, but the tech-heavy NASDAQ index skyrocketed by an incredible 86% during the same time period. However, Buffett did not participate in any of the investments made by these technology companies. He was quite positive that the increase in the market was due to nothing but rainbows and unicorns. He almost probably did not buy shares of internet businesses for Berkshire, as he allowed everyone else to make the easy money, and he was questioned about it. For many years during this time period, Buffett was plagued with self-doubt over his talents as an investor and the strategies he employed. The decline in the price of Berkshire's stock, which also occurred, provided the media with additional ammunition to support their assertion that Buffett had seen his greatest days. The criticism was harsh and unyielding throughout.

It is simple to be misunderstood, or even worse, made fun of, yet the Oracle maintained her composure. When asked about the time period in question, Buffett replied the following in an interview: "You can't do well in investing unless you think independently. The reality is that the fact that other individuals share your views does not make you right or incorrect. You are correct because the facts and rationale you presented are correct. At the end of the day, it's all that matters." Buffett was ultimately correct in his assessment. Investing was still about value; the industry hadn't become obsolete suddenly. The path to develop wealth over the long term was not discovered by throwing money at anything and everything that ended in '.com.' However, it is most likely that they were trying to get Buffett to hear and take the hits. There will be moments when it is difficult for you as well, but if you have built your investing philosophy effectively, now is the time to acquire the self-confidence and thick skin you need to continue with it.

Buffett has, on multiple occasions, shown that he is capable of withstanding the strain that comes from social situations. Even when the market dropped by 22.6% in a single day in October 1987, Warren Buffett did not flee the stock market out of fear. In a similar manner, he did not panic or sell his stock holdings when news surfaced about the huge accounting fraud that had been committed at Enron and other firms (in late 2001 and early 2002), which caused investors to mistrust management and the reported financial results. Almost immediately, significant scrutiny was placed on the executive ranks of every publicly traded company and business. Buffett took advantage of the conditions generated by all that nervousness and looked at the conditions caused by all that nervousness. He made the statement that "cash combined with courage in a time of crisis is priceless." It is feasible to put into effect the adage "Greedy when others are fearful and fearful when others are greedy," both when the market as a whole is declining as well as on the level of an individual company.

Buffett has been successful by targeting companies that are temporarily down because investors misunderstand or doubt their future earning potential and by jumping into the market and snapping up shares of many desirable businesses when everyone else seems to have run off, leaving cheap stocks scattered about like abandoned toys. Buffett has also been successful by targeting companies that are temporarily down because investors misunderstand or doubt their future earning potential. Buffett's position on dividends and stock splits is another example of how he maintains his independence in the face of intense criticism from his peers. Buffett has stated that Berkshire does not pay any dividends to its stockholders, with the exception of a single payment of $0.10

per share that was distributed in 1967. The explanation is straightforward: he is of the opinion that Berkshire stockholders would benefit more from him keeping the money rather than giving them a dividend in order to reinvest it in Berkshire's portfolio of totally owned and partially owned firms, rather than paying out a dividend to them. Although there are tax repercussions associated with paying dividends, both on the level of the company and on the level of the individual shareholder, Buffett does not consider this to be his primary concern.

Buffett believes that the most essential aspect of a company is how its resources are distributed. If you are able to effectively invest your capital into lucrative new business lines or into the improvement of existing business lines, then you shouldn't be paying a dividend. However, this is a very big "if," so you shouldn't count on it. If a company has reached maturity and is not expanding at a quick rate, and if management's ability to deploy capital is limited, then shareholders have the right to demand that the money be paid out to them in order to compensate for the likelihood that the stock price would not increase. However, in the case of Berkshire, we can all agree that Buffett is a master capital allocator, and it's a safe bet that he can do more with the excess money generated by the company's insurance operations than his shareholders could because he is one of the legends of investing. Berkshire's insurance operations generate a lot of extra money. However, certain investors and sectors of the market are dissatisfied with Buffett's approach since they want to get dividends as a source of income from their investments. On the other hand, it makes perfect sense and is totally in line with his opinions.

There is always the risk that Berkshire's enormous size would eventually catch up with it and create a situation in which paying out a dividend makes more sense than keeping all of the revenues for themselves. This is something that could happen at any time. However, that has not been the case so far. Buffett has been sounding the alarm for years about the drag that Berkshire's size has on its earnings, and at some point in the future, this could make it more difficult for him to rationally justify his current position on dividends. Also, Buffett has long been of the opinion that stock splits are a waste of time, money, and energy and that they should be avoided at all costs. In the event of a stock split, the total value of your shares will remain the same; however, the number of shares that you hold will increase. For example, if you bought 10 shares of Joshua shops at a price of $5 per share and the company split its stock 2-for-1, then you would possess 20 shares of Joshua stores at a price of $2.5 per share. In either case, the value of your investment is $50.

There are many different motivations for corporations to split their shares, but Buffett does not find any of those reasons to be particularly compelling. Some people believe that it is because they want to help create greater "liquidity" and make it simpler for more investors to purchase shares in the company. This is without a doubt one of the arguments that has been put out as a justification for Buffett to split the 'A' shares of Berkshire Hathaway. Because one share of Berkshire is currently selling for close to $438,000, the company's stock is priced out of reach for the vast majority of investors.

However, Buffett is of the opinion that splitting the stock of Berkshire would not be beneficial to either the company or its owners, and that it might even result in the formation of a group of shareholders that he considers to be unfavorable. Buffett wants Berkshire to have shareholders who are focused on the long term, and he also wants the price of Berkshire shares to be as close to reflective of the company's underlying value as feasible. If the company is split, it will make it more likely that irrational stock movements will occur as a result of additional speculative shareholders who are only interested in the short term.

But around the middle of the 1990s, Buffet was put in an awkward position regarding the stock split issue. Investment firms were aware that many more people still desired to own a piece of Berkshire Hathaway but were unable to do so due to financial constraints. As a result, these firms came up with the idea to buy shares of Berkshire, divide them up, and then sell the resulting smaller units to the general public while charging hefty fees. As a result, in 1996, Buffett established a second class of Berkshire shares in order to eliminate what he considered to be an inefficient and unjust method of profiting from Berkshire's success. These 'B' shares had voting rights equal to 1/200 of a 'A' share's and were valued at 1/30 of the value of a 'A' share. However, in early 2010, the 'B' shares of Berkshire were divided 1/50 in order to facilitate an easier decision-making process for the shareholders of Burlington Northern. This was done in light of the fact that Berkshire had declared that it was intending to finish the takeover of Burlington Northern by the end of 2009.

Buffett made it easy for Burlington stockholders to pick Berkshire shares rather than cash by lowering the share price for them and avoiding difficult tax ramifications. Burlington shareholders had the option of either receiving cash or Berkshire stock as their dividend payment. This action also made it possible for Berkshire to take Burlington Northern's place in the S&P 500; prior to this point, Berkshire had not been included on this list. It is noteworthy to notice that Buffett has not changed his mind on the absurdity of stock splits, which brings up an interesting point. He didn't come to the conclusion that everyone else was right about stock splits all of a sudden; rather, he made the decision to do what he did with the 'B' shares because he was looking out for the best interests of tiny, individual investors. Buffett has a high value on his reputation, which is still another reason why he is not likely to give in to the pressure that is being applied by society. Buffett will not become involved in something if there is even a remote possibility that it could tarnish his reputation. He once imparted this wisdom to his eldest son, which has since become famous: "It takes twenty years to build a reputation, and five minutes to ruin it." If you give some thought to that, you'll find that you approach things differently.

Buffett has a firm belief in something he refers to as the "inner scorecard." To put it simply, it's a framework for living your life in accordance with the guidelines and principles that you've established for yourself, as opposed to basing your actions on whether or not other people will approve of you. Naturally, this incorporates Buffett's decision-making process regarding his finances. You have to block out the outside world and live by the scorecard you have in your head. If you want to be a successful investor, you will need to learn how to navigate the market on your own. You can learn from the masters, like Buffett did and like you are doing now by reading this book, but in the end, you have to establish your own system for investing. Buffett is a good example of someone who did this. Then you need to be consistent with your approach. There will be periods of difficulty, but you should not give up on your principles at this point in life. You are free to pose as many questions as you like, and then to take whatever action you deem appropriate after doing so. This aspect of Buffett's temperament is one of the primary reasons he has been able to achieve the kind of success he has, and he has had a significant amount of time to work on perfecting it. Therefore, start

your adventure, persevere in it, and
preserve your strength.

Principal Applications Of Option Trading And Investing

Options are used in one of two primary ways by professional options investors: either to reduce the risk associated with other investments or to place a wager on the direction that the market is going to be heading in the near future.

Speculation refers to betting on the market, and options traders who are able to read the market can use it to make money regardless of which direction the market is moving in. Speculators need to know not only how the market is going to move, but also the pace at which it is going to move. This is why speculation can be responsible for massive financial swings in both directions. Speculators need to know how the market is going to move, but also the speed at which it is going to move. The fact that each option represents 100 shares contributes to the market's volatility because it means that even relatively minor shifts in the underlying stock can result in large movement in the options that are tied to that stock.

Using options as a hedge against other assets is not risky at all, in contrast to speculating, which can be risky. In this case, the trader acquires options, which are effectively a form of insurance that safeguards the trader's other assets that they have made. Having a put option gives the trader the ability to assure that they will at least get their money back if the stock price of the underlying stock drops significantly. This is particularly helpful if the trader's other investment is a stock that has a high level of volatility because having a put option gives the trader the ability to guarantee that they will have this outcome. In a similar vein, if the value of the stock that the option is based on drastically increases, the trader can choose to let the option expire and will only be responsible for the fees associated with the options trade. Traders can engage in potentially dangerous but potentially rewarding deals thanks to this method, which allows them to safeguard themselves to the greatest extent feasible.

Be aware of what can be expected.

If you want to be successful in trading on a consistent basis, the very first thing you are going to need to concentrate on is distancing yourself from the process emotionally so that you can make rational decisions. Your objective will be to devise a trading strategy (covered in chapter 4) that you will be able to adhere to in every aspect. This will make it simpler for you to make decisions that are in your best interests, even if a number of your recent transactions have not been successful and your feelings are beginning to get the better of you.

However, the first thing you need to do in order to successfully complete this procedure is to have a reasonable expectation of what to anticipate from your first attempt at trading options. This requires you to let go of whatever delusions you may have, such as the belief that you will become wealthy after making only a few trades, or that you don't need to do any study but can instead rely on your intuition, in order to get the kinds of outcomes over the long run that you are hoping to achieve. Additionally, you will want to begin by keeping a journal of the feelings you feel throughout each phase of the trade in question so that you can look back on them later on and get a clear sense of when you are likely to experience which sort of emotion and why. This will allow you to look back on them and get a clear concept of when you are likely to experience certain emotions and why.

Because new options traders, as a norm, have the expectation that everything will always go according to plan, this is the primary source of worry that they experience when trading options. As a matter of fact, this will never be the case one hundred percent of the time, and even a tried and true technique will never produce perfect results. Because of this, investing in options is considered to be riskier than investing in some other sorts of investments, such as those you might choose. If, instead of focusing on whether or not each transaction produced money, you focus on following your method to the letter each time and not letting emotion or the results of the prior trades distract you from following through in the best way possible, you will find it simpler to accept this fact.

Traders who are successful in options trading are those that adhere to their systems religiously and rely on the fact that the system's average returns are greater than 50 percent as a guarantee that they will generate a profit over the course of their careers. When you keep this information in mind, it will be much simpler for you to manage losing trades in the moment, and it will also be much simpler for you to choose dependable options trades over those that provide high margins for both risk and profit. It is vital to bear in mind that the longer you exercise restraint, the simpler it will be to practice it in the future. Although it will be easier to think about obtaining this attitude than really doing it in the beginning, it will be easier to think about achieving it in the long run.

Developing A Strategy For Penny Stocks: Some Pointers

First and foremost, you must have a healthy respect for the risk that is involved. It's possible that this will develop over time, but you should never disregard it. However, you should appreciate it and not be afraid of it at the same time. Make every effort to steer clear of such dangers whenever you can. In the long term, it simply ends up being a superior option overall.

Make sure that your goals are very clear. Be as specific as possible because it will be much simpler for you to formulate an actionable strategy the more you know about the end goal you are trying to achieve.

It is advisable that a newbie begin with a modest amount. No matter how knowledgeable you are or how much experience you have, beginning with a modest investment and working your way up will help you mitigate a significant amount of risk and cushion the blow of financial setbacks when they inevitably occur. In addition, beginning with a modest budget, particularly at the outset, helps prevent the accumulation of large problems and debt by ensuring that these issues aren't incurred in the first place.

Choosing a mentor is another fantastic thing you can do to accelerate your learning process. You should prioritize finding a mentor who has really traveled the same road you intend to go in the future. The mentor can be of assistance by preventing many of the errors that you could make and revealing to you several techniques that you may not have considered previously. To reiterate, it is in your best interest to acquire the ability to think independently;

nevertheless, no one ever suggested that you are prohibited from receiving any kind of assistance.

Do not put yourself in an unnecessary position of risk by forcing a deal simply because you believe that a trade ought to take place. It is a sign that you are doing something incorrectly or possibly acting a little too hurriedly if you need to coerce a trade. Instead, you should wait for the deal to come to you, and you should never make any judgments on a trade that significantly deviates from your initial trading plan unless you have a good reason that can be substantiated.

When Day Trading, Things to Keep an Eye Out For in Stocks

It is common knowledge that working with penny stocks requires more of a hands-on approach than other types of stock trading. Because of this, if you want to profit from the more volatile market that persists throughout the day, you are going to have to become skilled in the art of day trading.

When you first begin day trading in penny stocks and as you advance in your career in this market, there are a few things you should keep an eye out for. These are some pointers that can help you locate the potentially most lucrative trade that takes place on that day:

To begin, it acts as a catalyst. It just so happens that news is one of the key drivers of stocks to go upwards or downwards in a relatively short amount of time. Because of this, it is extremely crucial to stay current on the news and trends without having any sort of bias. On the other hand, if you are able to forecast a trend, you will be able to find yourself ahead of the curve, which is the scenario that you want to find yourself in.

In addition to this, you should be on the lookout for a stock with a low float. In this type of ownership structure, the majority of the shares are typically held by "insiders" as well as "actual major investors." This indicates that there is a restricted quantity of stocks, and the shareholders' ability to sell is also extremely restricted. This, in the end, indicates that demand and supply are functioning effectively, which results in the likelihood of several price shifts taking place in that market.

It goes without saying that having the ability to recognize a killer chart pattern is great. When you have reached this point, you have found a pattern that has a potential trend that you can leverage to your advantage. Your day trading will profit from your grasp of patterns and chart readings, which is why it is so extremely vital to learn chart patterns.

Chart patterns may be found on price charts.

Obviously, another thing that you need to keep an eye out for is evidence of increased trade volume. When this occurs, you will witness an increase in the number of shares being exchanged over a relatively brief period of time. This is typically a significant indication that there is a lot of buzz about a certain stock, and that traders are flocking in to receive their share of the strong gains.

Alternative Public Blockchains

Even at the most fundamental protocol layer, which is the foundation upon which all other apps are constructed, the new entrant will find a huge menu of blockchain choices when they first delve into the area. These Bitcoin alternatives were, for the most part, presented as purported upgrades to the original cryptocurrency, which necessitated the creation of a separate blockchain. In this chapter, we will talk about some of the available alternatives, as well as at least one of the purported flaws, inefficiencies, or confinements that they claim to improve upon. This section will also be a beneficial source of knowledge and understanding about many of the larger capitalization blockchain networks that the reader may also see referenced in the media and listed on token exchanges. This will occur as a byproduct of the process described above.

The first criticism is that Bitcoin is unsuitable for any purpose other than financial transactions.

Ethereum (ETH)

The desire of some members of the community to do more with Bitcoin, whose scripting language had some limitations – and was thus not Turing complete – and was meant to primarily deal with some straightforward true/false evaluations of spending conditions, also known as "just make payments," led to the creation of Ethereum. A programming language that, in essence, was "Turing complete," and that, as a result, was capable of being used to code and run programs of arbitrary complexity, such as smart contracts. Nearly all of the programming languages that are now being used are considered to be Turing complete. Solidity is the name of the programming language that is used only for coding Ethereum's applications.

In order to standardize particular categories of smart contracts, developers will submit a format proposal to the community in the form of a "Ethereum Request for Comment" (ERC), which stands for Ethereum Request for Comment. In point of fact, the majority of Initial Coin Offerings (ICOs), which will be discussed in greater depth in the following chapter on regulation, were conducted using an ERC-20 token. On the other hand, the game Cryptokitties, which generates one-of-a-kind, non-fungible digital art, was conducted using an ERC-721 token.

An example of the pseudocode used for an ERC-20 token may be found below. You will find various lines in it that allow for specificity in the process of establishing a new token, such as the total supply, name, and ticker symbol. These lines may be found in it. The remaining lines make it possible to perform actions such as checking the balance of many wallet addresses at the same time and transferring funds from one wallet to another.

In the case of Ethereum, the efforts of the miner are calculated as a function of the number of steps in the contract that require validation. The bigger the number of validations, the more work that is required of the miner, and as a result, the miner will charge a higher fee for their services.

The Tokens That Cannot Be Exchanged

The non-fungible token, often known as NFT for short, is an unusual unit of data that cannot be exchanged with other units. It is kept in what is known as a digital ledger, which is recorded in a blockchain. It is possible for non-fungible tokens to be associated with easily reproducible elements such as audio, video, photo, and other types of digital assets. Every piece of data that has been saved has been authenticated and given a certificate. The public proof of ownership that is provided is validated thanks to the utilization of blockchain technology. The person who owns the non-fungible tokens does not have exclusive access to the copies of the actual files. The owner has the ability to make copies and distribute them in the same manner that files are distributed.

The fact that non-fungible tokens cannot be exchanged for other currencies is what sets them apart from cryptocurrencies like bitcoin. The data unit is able to be kept on a distributed digital ledger known as a blockchain, which enables it to be bought, sold, and traded. The NFT is analogous to a specific physical item, such as a file or a digital asset, and can be thought of in the same way. In addition, a license will be granted in order to allow the asset to be utilized for a certain activity. In digital marketplaces, a license that allows one to use and display an item can be bought, sold, or traded. The cryptographic tokens and the non-fungible tokens are virtually identical to one another; but, unlike Bitcoin, NTFS cannot be exchanged for one another, which is why it is not fungible. Bitcoins are indivisible; their values cannot be differentiated in any way. On the other hand, a single NTFS file might represent a diverse variety of underlying assets. When blockchains string the cryptographic hash records with sets of characters that identify data assets in previously owned records, NTFS is produced. As a result, a series of data blocks that are capable of being recognized will be crafted. This procedure verifies that each and every component of a digital file has been given an authenticated status. The owner of the digital file will supply a digital signature that can be accessed in order to verify who is in possession of the NFT.

The non-fungible tokens have some sort of relationship to the Metaverse. With the use of this token, creators of avatars, digital arts, musical content, and even videos can publish their work in the Metaverse.

The digital arts

Because it can use blockchain technology to confirm the signature and ownership of NTFS, thus many artists have started using it. NTFS is a network file system. Because of the NTFS, so many artists have been able to practically sell their works.

It is possible to use Games NTFS in place of in-game assets such as digital plots of land, with the end result being that the user, and not the game creator, will have control over these assets. It is not necessary to obtain authorization from the person who developed the game in order to trade assets on platforms and marketplaces that are operated by third parties.

Worlds in cyberspace

Users of certain virtual worlds, such as Sandbox, Decentraland, and cryptocvoxels, are granted the ability to construct galleries in which they can exhibit their works of art and in-game possessions. You may even put up virtual real estate for auction with it in different games.

People now have a greater number of chances than ever before to tokenize and publish their albums using non-fungible tokens thanks to advancements in music technology and blockchain.

The Big Banks

The reputation of the nation's largest banks has taken a hit in recent years. In the recent past, there have been a number of occurrences that have contributed to an overall increase in mistrust among the general public. This mistrust is, to a large extent, warranted; nevertheless, a portion of it may be founded on falsehoods. Whatever the circumstances may be, we are not going to be discussing it at this time. Depending on a number of critical considerations, banking institutions may constitute an excellent opportunity for financial investments.

Banks perform a function for society that is extremely important and will never be eliminated because of its importance.

The business model of a bank is one that is not overly complicated to grasp. They make their profit by collecting cash deposits from customers who open a variety of accounts, and they invest this money in a variety of high-interest lending products, such as mortgages.

Because the price of many bank stocks is so low, an investor can get in with a relatively small amount of money. Investing does not require you to take out a loan or a second mortgage on your home.

You might want to consider include some bank shares in your portfolio of investments. The following is a list of the three various kinds of banks that exist:

Commercial banks are the most common sort of bank, and they are the establishments in which customers typically go to make deposits as well as a variety of other types of transactions.

Investment banks: Organizations will typically retain the services of investment banks in order to assist them with complicated financial transactions. For individuals, corporations, and governments, as well as providing guidance on mergers, acquisitions, and corporate restructuring, this category of banking encompasses the process of raising capital. Unlike retail and commercial banks, investment banks do not accept deposits from customers.

Banks that fall under this category are known as universal banks, and they offer the same services as commercial and investment banks. The use of universal banks is significantly more widespread throughout Europe. Because of the numerous constraints, its expansion in the United States has been somewhat sluggish.

Although they have the potential to be profitable, investing in bank stocks is not a foolproof plan. When conducting an assessment of bank stocks, there are a few factors to take into consideration. It is essential for there to be good loans available at the financial institutions. Poor lending practices in the past were a major contributing factor in many of the financial crises that occurred in the past. Consider the bank risk measurements that are presented in the following list.

Non-performing loan ratio, often known as the NPL ratio: These are debts that are at least 90 days past due and are on the verge of going into default. If you have a portfolio that is strong, having a large number of these loans is not a good sign. To determine this ratio, take the entire amount of money that is owed on loans that are not performing and divide that sum by the total number of loans that are still due. After that, multiply this number by 100 to get the final answer. For instance, if a financial institution has 7 billion in non-performing loans but 950 billion in total loans, the institution has a ratio of 0.7%. It is reasonable to feel uneasy about anything with a percentage that is greater than two percent. When the number of nonperforming loans (NPL) is high, it indicates that financial institutions are making an excessive number of loans to persons who do not meet the criteria for receiving them. Even while the borrower is largely to blame for this, the lender's severe recklessness should not be overlooked.

Protection against risky loans: as was said earlier, there is no guarantee that a loan will be repaid in full. Loans that have not been repaid are recorded, and the provisions for loan loss or coverage of bad loans are referred to. The coverage for bad loans is calculated by taking the allowance for loan loss provisions and dividing that number by the total amount of loans that are not performing as expected. After being multiplied by 100, the final figure will be expressed as a percentage. For instance, if a financial institution had an outstanding non-performing loan balance of 6.5 billion dollars and had put aside 10 billion dollars for loan loss provisions, the financial institution would have 153% coverage for bad loans. It is a positive indicator if the financial institution has a larger quantity of money set aside for the coverage of bad loans than the actual amount of bad loans it has.

The term "net charge-offs" refers to a declaration made by the lending bank that the amount of the loan that was provided will most likely not be repaid. In most cases, they will make this announcement after the debtor has gone approximately six months without making any payments. The NCO is calculated by taking the NCO's total loans, dividing that number by the total loans, and then multiplying that result by 100. For instance, if the entire amount of loans is 900 billion dollars and the net charge-off is 4 billion, then the rate of total net charge-offs is 0.44%. Comparison to the sector average throughout the relevant time period is the most effective method for evaluating this number. When the economy is going through a rough patch, fewer debts are paid off.

When you first begin investing, large banks might be a formidable competitor for you. You may leverage them to your advantage in significant ways if you understand how they function. A lot of individuals view banks as the adversary. You are not need to have the same experience as this.

After all, the term "value investing" was coined for this strategy; there is little purpose in putting money into a stock that is already significantly overpriced. If you knew that the value of the home was just $300,000, you probably wouldn't buy it for $500,000, would you? The same guiding idea is applicable to stock trading.

If you want to be a successful value investor like Warren Buffett, you should only invest in stocks that have an intrinsic value that is higher than its current market price. In other words, you should only buy firms that are undervalued relative to their potential earnings.

This would imply that you anticipate a rise in the price of the stock over the course of time, with the market price naturally correcting itself towards the stock's intrinsic value, so providing you with the opportunity for significant capital gains.

It is inevitable that there may be circumstances in which the price of a stock will skyrocket well above its fundamental worth (for example, consider KO), but when this occurs, it is the result of investors' excessive self-assurance. For instance, The Coca-Cola Company has shown that it has a low current ratio (which indicates that it has a lot of debt) and inadequate earnings growth (which indicates that it is not becoming more profitable). The market's suggested prediction that the company will expand its earnings by 12% each year does not seem to be justified by the shown potential it possesses. Although there is no assurance of profit, it is still possible to earn real capital gains by investing in equities of this type, albeit with a much smaller margin of safety. It is impossible to predict when the market will bring the market price of the company back in line with its intrinsic worth.

Absolutely, he does. In point of fact, it is one of the largest holdings in Berkshire Hathaway's portfolio, accounting for 8.97% of the company's total assets and containing an astounding 400 MILLION shares. However, this does not imply that we should mindlessly copy Buffett's investment portfolio. If you examine more closely, you'll notice that he hasn't purchased any further KO shares in the past few years.

The majority of his 400 million shares were acquired after the stock market crash that occurred in 1987. At that time, KO was trading at $2.45 per share, which is a significant savings when compared to its current price of $42.70 per share. Because he bought the shares at a time when it was trading at a discount, Warren Buffett now possesses a share of a company that is grossly overpriced. And he maintains his ownership of it due to the fact that it offers a respectable dividend return. In the third chapter, we will show you how to select stocks from Buffett's portfolio that are appropriate for your own investment strategy.

What You Need To Know To Start Investing In The Stock Market

Stocks are widely regarded as the most common type of investment vehicle used today by financial professionals. The primary reason for this is that anyone may set up a brokerage account and buy stocks. In this chapter, you will become familiar with the fundamental concepts and words associated with stock investing. You will also get knowledge on the many methods of analysis that you will need to apply if you are making decisions regarding investments. At the conclusion of this book, you will be presented with a number of the most successful investment ideas now available on the stock market.

The Necessary Particulars Regarding Stocks

Experts consider stocks to be either securities or equities. This is due to the fact that when you buy a stock from a firm, you are effectively purchasing a share or a portion of the ownership of that company. That translates to the fact that you will have a stake in the ownership of some businesses.

There are Two Varieties of Stocks.

Common stocks and preferred stocks are the two categories of equities that are available. On the stock market, the most frequently traded securities are called common stocks. They are a representation of a share of ownership in the company and grant the holder the right to vote on issues relating to the company. People who possess common stocks have a chance of receiving dividends, but this is contingent on whether or not the management decides to make certain financial decisions.

On the other hand, preferred stocks provide good protection against abrupt price swings. This is the primary rationale behind the decision made by the vast majority of conservative investors to purchase preferred stocks. The principal benefit that comes along with owning this type of stock is that the payment of dividends to owners is NEARLY GUARANTEED to take place.

Comprehending The Contents Of The Balance Sheet

When it comes to conducting an analysis of financial data, the significance of the balance sheet cannot be emphasized. Let's have a look at the various parts that make it up.

Constituents of the Financial Statement

Accounting for businesses is focused entirely on determining the connections that exist between a company's resources and the environments in which those resources originated. To put it simply, resources are assets that an organization makes use of in order to achieve goals such as increased profit and revenue, increased brand awareness, and so on. These assets can be obtained by either the financial contributions of the company's shareholders or through the taking out of loans. The equation that summarizes all of this is as follows: Assets are equal to liabilities plus the equity held by the owners.

Let's define the components so that you can have a better understanding of that equation, shall we?

• The resources that are owned by the company and that it has access to for the purpose of producing and selling its goods and services are referred to as its assets. Investments, cash, inventory, customer-owned receivables, buildings, inventory, land, equipment, and other intangible assets are some examples of business-essential intangible assets. The company is the legal owner of the assets in question.

• Liabilities are assets that are not owned by the company, but rather are borrowed from other entities or financed by those entities. These consist of money that are owed to various suppliers, as well as long term and short term borrowings, and so on. The debts that are owing by the company are referred to as its liabilities.

• Owners' equity refers to the portion of the company's total assets that has been contributed by the owners of the company. This concept is also known as owners' capital, book value, stockholders' equity, and shareholders' equity. Additionally, it is sometimes referred to as net worth. This includes the capital donated by stockholders as well as any gains from the company's previous operations that have been retained, sometimes known as retained earnings.

A balance sheet must always be in perfect equilibrium. To put it another way, each and every dollar that is spent on assets and each and every dollar that is donated as part of the liabilities, or additional money from the owners, needs to be equivalent.

It is common practice to compile balance sheets after a predetermined period of time, typically at the conclusion of the fiscal year and the conclusion of each fiscal quarter. The balance sheet is a necessary consolidation that is required because the majority of organizations will almost certainly have a significant number of accounts. As a value investor, the last thing you need is to be required to look through a gazillion accounts that have been set up by the company for every form of asset and inventory, and these accounts may be located in any one of a number of different countries. By condensing everything onto a single page, the balance sheet saves you a lot of trouble.

When reviewing a company's balance sheet, value investors should keep an eye out for the following three items:

• What exactly is included in the categories of assets, liabilities, and owners' equity? It is not a positive sign for the business if there is insufficient cash but an excessive amount of inventory.

• An analysis of the most recent developments in the industry. A negative situation exists when there is an insufficient amount of owners' equity and an excessive amount of debt.

• The degree to which the proclaimed values accurately represent the real values held by the organization.

You will be given information regarding the present state of the company's finances and health. A balance sheet is not reliable as a tool for forecasting the future. When an analyst has to determine whether or not the figures on a balance sheet are accurate, they turn to established ratios. These ratios allow the analyst to quickly and readily compare the subject company to other businesses in its industry.

Fund for Future Education Expenses

A 529 plan is a particularly specific kind of investment fund that can be used for college savings. It is only allowed to be used for costs associated with receiving a college degree, it is governed by the individual states as well as the District of Columbia, and it is permitted by the Internal Revenue Service. I made the decision to add the 529 savings plan because I believe that one of the most important aspects of investing is to plan for the future in order to alleviate some of the stress associated with providing for one's family. A college education has become somewhat of a requirement in today's labor markets, and a college savings plan will be of tremendous assistance to you in bearing the financial load of this obligation.

There are two different types of 529 plans, and your state may offer both of them, just one of them, or neither of them at all. Both pre-paid plans and traditional savings plans for college can be purchased now. There are currently more states that provide the college savings plan, and it is likely that you will use this form of investment if you decide to establish a 529 plan for yourself. The primary distinction between these two options is that with a pre-paid account, a student is able to begin making payments for a specific university immediately, using the amount that the university will charge in 2017. These payments are normally made on a per-credit-hour basis, and they are typically only accepted at schools that are run by the state. You may, for instance, begin paying for the credit hours that your child intends to spend in the future at a number of state institutions if you start paying for them now. After that, they are free to choose to attend any state institution of their choosing, and these payments will follow them there. If your child does not attend a state school, you will either be required to write off the investment entirely or pay significant penalties in order to withdraw any money from the plan. It is also important to note that the pre-paid plan can only be utilized for the purchase of college credits, and not for room and board or any other fees associated with attending the institution.

The general savings plan gives you more flexibility about how you can spend the money, but it also does not lower the fees to the same extent that the other plans do. This money can be used on a state school or a private institution, and money deposited into an account will be disbursed with a severe tax reduction when your child is ready to go to school. State schools and private institutions both accept this money. If it turns out that you do not have any children who go to college, you may be able to get your money back, but there will be a significant penalty attached to doing so. It varies from state to state in terms of how severe of an effect this penalty has. The money in this fund can also be used to pay for your own education; it does not necessarily have to go toward a degree at a college or university. For example, it could be implemented in a program for job retraining or utilized at a vocational school.

The education expenses of your children are the only sort of return that can be received from a 529 plan. The ever-increasing costs are a cause for concern, and you can anticipate that the cost of attending college will continue to go up as having a college degree becomes an increasingly important factor in landing a good job. If you are certain that you will have children who attend college, you should do some research on how the 529 plan works in your state and open an account as soon as possible. When it comes to saving money for higher education, this is hands down the most effective fund that you can establish. The value of money held in a 529 fund rises at a rapid rate, and the tax breaks afforded to savers through this type of account are among the most advantageous that the government provides. There is no reason for you not to make advantage of this fund, as it is one that virtually all wealthy people in the United States use to pay for their children's education.

Why Should You Care About This?

You might believe that doing drugs is a calling, or maybe you just can't wait to get away from this place. Money won't solve all of your problems, but it will at least give you options to consider. Assuming that your goal is to abandon medication, the following guidelines can be of assistance to you in getting there. Assuming that you actively participate in the healing process, you will be able to shape your professional life in such a way that it aligns with the factors that initially drew you to the field of medicine. Having a guide is helpful to ensure that this is carried out in the most efficient manner possible.

My primary objective is to serve as that helper and work alongside you to effect positive change in both your personal and professional life. This book will provide you with the tools necessary to construct a pipeline that is continuously generating automated money. This pipeline will help you overcome any obstacles that stand between where you are now and where you need to go in the future. We will construct the pipeline in concert with one another.

We will piece together the architecture that will support your pipeline with each successive component that is installed. Your pipeline is supported by a series of columns, each of which addresses a plain yet fruitful idea that contributes to your progression toward fully automated revenue. These pictures are the result of 25 years of commitment on my part, and they were achieved in the most challenging way imaginable by learning from mistakes, experimenting, and remaining committed to teaching.

Observing these guidelines will help you avoid making the same mistakes that I did on your path to financial freedom and emancipation from the rat race. You will be able to make the life you have generally dreamt of living if you have a very much established pipeline of automatic revenue. This will ease some financial anxiety and provide you the option to make more money.

It is my hope that all specialists will take the time to read this book. And after that, for every single legal counsel, designer, and sales rep—in fact, every single expert of any kind—to do the same thing as well. The goal is to have a large number of people who are financially independent and have the power to make positive changes in the world.

While some will need to continue in their chosen calling but with less pressure and impediment, some individuals may choose to quit their jobs prematurely so that they can participate in their lives. In any event, other people will channel their efforts into something new, such as reversing the effects of cancerous development or making life better for other people.

It is my sincere hope that the knowledge I have obtained as a working business visionary may be of some use to you in achieving your goals, regardless of what those goals may be. Also, assuming that more people work and live their lives in their own unique ways, such as you do, won't that make this world a better and more happier place?

8. Stay firm in your convictions.

The next step, which some would argue is the most essential, is to remain consistent with one's efforts, possibly for decades.

You will learn how to become wealthy by utilizing all of the information that has been presented to you, but if you are not willing to commit to these methods for the long haul, your efforts will be in vain. According to research that made the assumption of a median family income and invested conservatively, it would take an average of 61 years to accumulate enough wealth to become a billionaire.

This number may seem disappointing, but it actually demonstrates how much longer it would take the average person to become affluent. The encouraging news is that you may be able to cut down on that period of time by increasing both your income and your assets. It is possible for a large number of people to become millionaires within the next ten years if they have a salary that is average or above and little or no debt.

Also, keep in mind that the benefits to both your life and your finances that you will experience along the way will make the journey well worth the effort, even if it takes you a longer time to become affluent.

To summarize, becoming wealthy is a goal that must be pursued over the course of a long period of time and may take the majority of your life to accomplish. It is most likely that the achievement of your goal will come down to whether or not you are dedicated and persistent in your efforts.

A Few Parting Thoughts

For those of you who are interested in learning how to amass a lot of wealth, the path to financial success is actually fairly simple.

First, you should establish a goal for yourself, then calculate your number, then educate yourself, and finally, you should become familiar with your current financial status. After you've laid the framework, the next step is to devise a plan to boost your income, eliminate your debt, and start investing. In conclusion, you should get ready to implement this strategy throughout the next many decades.

I can guarantee that the changes you make now will make a positive impact on the rest of your life, even if you don't end up being filthy rich.

Comparing Working To Investing

When people first start becoming involved in land investing, one of the things that may be the most mysterious to new investors is the actual amount of labor that will be required for various strategies of land investment.

Let's break this down into its component parts by distinguishing between working and contributing.

When it comes to investing, having cash on hand is the means to the benefit.

Putting in effort: labor is the route to financial reward.

When you invest in stocks, you hand over your cash, you don't do anything besides maybe occasionally look at the stock prices, and then at some point in the future, you withdraw your money from the account. Pure speculation is what you have done in order to gain the cash from your corporation security.

92

Since you don't actually get any work done, the advantages are all due to the speculating in and of itself.

The purchase of land notes would be comparable to this. Because you contribute money to the note but do not perform any work, any advantage you derive from that enterprise is attributable only to the act of speculating itself.

The majority of people that become involved in land contributing meaning do so with the intention of achieving the same objective - a venture. They are looking for ways to make a profit off of their money. They are required to invest a certain amount of money into a business initiative or opportunity, and they must realize a profit in the form of additional financial capital as a result of that investment. That is, for the most part, how a speculation works, and it is reasonable to assume that this is the goal that individuals have in mind when they choose to invest in real estate as a form of business plan.

However, things have the potential to go rather awry when people aren't aware that certain land investment strategies demand an insane amount of work. Work is not anything to be ashamed of, but it is not the same thing as putting money into something.

In the case of certain land investing techniques, the amount of money you make from your investment is directly proportional to the amount of labour you put in. If you choose to invest your time and effort into a business enterprise, the advantages you reap will be a combination of 1) the return on your investment, and 2) compensation for the time and effort you put in (labor). Take, for example, the act of flipping a property. You invest in a distressed property and acquire the recovery as an asset. This is your opportunity to make some money. However, at that time, you will be responsible for recovering the residence on your own. You devote time and effort into mending and further improving items, as well as supervising people who are hired. Imagine that over the course of a period of four months, you put in a total of 200 hours working on the rehabilitation of this property. If you are telling the truth about the profit you make on the flip, then you should consider some of that profit to be payment for the two hundred hours that you spent working on the project, and the rest of that profit should be considered to be the actual profit from the venture, rather than considering the entire thing to be profit from the investment.

It is important to determine the source of your financial gain for two reasons: a) you want to make sure that you are earning the target amount on your investment, and b) you need to know in advance what kind of time and work requirement this particular investment is going to require so that you can determine whether or not it is feasible for you to do it.

Every business model will call for a different kind of effort to be put in. As a starting point for your consideration, below are some of the most well-known approaches to land speculation:

When it comes to wholesaling, it's all labour and no investment.

To flip a house requires equal parts work and investment.[8]

The management of rental properties involves equal parts labour and investment.

Employing property managers for rental properties results in little more labor but a significant increase in investment.

notes and REITS: no labor required, 100% investment return

I'll ask this again: what impact does this have? Considering that you need to weigh the potential consequences of working for your businesses against those of:

availability hazard tolerances expert level premium level availability hazard tolerances expert level

For my part, I have a lot of access to resources and a high tolerance for risk, which enables me to have the option of going completely wild with my assumptions. My level of expertise isn't terrible, but it's also not fantastic. I'm not very good at doing specific bits of work myself, but I'm very good at project management, so I could supervise employees for hire if I needed to. My level of expertise isn't terrible, but it's also not terrific. My advantage level, on the other hand, is where I fall short of expectations. To put it gently, saying that I do not have absolutely any premium in dealing with my speculations would be stretching the truth. I am dissatisfied, I do not take pleasure in supervising project workers, I try to avoid getting up early to meet project workers, I like to work as little as possible for my money, and I despise the idea of being secured or required to be there at a given time.

When I observe such a high level of mindfulness, I am able to begin more easily evaluating which business practices could be most suitable for me. This evaluation will be different for each person, and it is important that you are honest with yourself during the process.

 In that case, you run the risk of quickly coming to despise your assets.

The Keys To Being Successful In Day Trading

When engaging in day trading, it is crucial to have trading methods at your disposal that will assist you in turning a profit the majority of the time. If you do not have any trustworthy go-to tactics, you can end yourself having to speculate about what you should do. Therefore, the most effective strategy for getting forward in the game is to always have a good grasp of what options are available to you.

In this chapter, we are going to take a look at some fundamental tactics that can assist you in making money while also assisting you in gaining an advantage over your competitors. It is important to keep in mind that the average success rate for investors is between 50 and 60 percent. In most cases, investors come out on top of their trades. However, I ask that you do your best to prepare to fail. Therefore, the most important aspect of your strategy is deciding what to do in the event that your plans are unsuccessful. The manner in which you respond to challenges like these will determine how successful an investor you will become.

Essential Methodologies

You really have to adhere to these fundamental strategies if you want to be successful. They are advice that apply to all aspects of trading, and you can put them into practice whenever you decide to initiate a deal. In addition, these methods are tried and true approaches that have the potential to protect you from the errors that inexperienced investors frequently make. Therefore, make sure that you always put them at the forefront of your mind whenever you are investing in stocks.

Managing one's finances

The administration of your investment funds is what is meant by the term "money management." You may use this strategy to help you build discipline in your asset allocation decisions, and it can be quite useful. You are responsible for adhering to the following two primary rules.

The cardinal principle. The purpose of this regulation is to ensure that individual trades do not consume an excessive amount of capital. According to the "golden rule," you should never put more than two percent of your total investment capital into a single deal at any given time. You have the ability to invest the entirety of your capital; however, it is not recommended that you do so in a single transaction. Please bear in mind that the greater the amount of money that you invest in a single trade, the higher the associated risk.

Increasing our bets. When investors suffer a financial loss, they often feel the urge to make up for it by putting in twice as much money in their subsequent trades. This is done to make up for the money they lost in the prior trade. This method puts you in a very precarious position. It has the potential to cause you to lose a lot more money than you did before. For instance, if you placed a trade and lost $100, you might be tempted to place another $200 in the same transaction. On the other hand, if something were to go wrong, you stand to lose an additional $200 on top of the initial $100. Therefore, it is in your best interest to stick to your strategy. You will one day be able to make up for your losses.

The art of market timing

The beginning and the end of the trading session are typically times when there is a greater volume of trading activity than at any other time during the session. Therefore, this is the kind of situation in which you need to throw yourself into the fray. A rush of activity can be seen throughout the first two hours of the trading day. An HFT approach can be flawlessly put into action in this location. Within a very brief time frame of two hours, you have the opportunity to engage in many trades. A number of traders are capable of opening and closing their trades in a matter of seconds. The same holds true for the final two hours and fifteen minutes before the market closes. At this point, it would be wise to close out any open positions that you have. However, you need to be careful since the market downturn that occurs just before the close of each trading day has the potential to reduce the amount of money you make.

Administration of Time

Being reliable is essential to effective time management. Putting forth effort to improve your skills on a daily basis is highly recommended. If you just glance at your trading platform once or twice a week, you could be startled to find that your results aren't what you expected them to be. This is especially true if you only look at charts occasionally. As a consequence of this, maintaining a constant commitment with regard to the quantity of time you invest is essential.

In addition to the time they devote to research, the majority of successful day traders spend between two and three hours a day actually trading on their platform. When you have a full-service account, a significant portion of the research is carried out on your behalf. Therefore, in order to determine where you want to put your trades, all you need to do is read through your news feed. After that, you will be able to configure the system so that it does everything for you.

Payment of dividends

Are you looking for a source of consistent income? When a company is making such a significant amount of money, it may choose to give some of that money back to its shareholders in the form of a dividend. This does result in price fluctuations, depending on whether they choose to raise or lower the dividend, but in general, well-established and reputable businesses won't have any problems with this scenario.

Generally speaking, dividends are disbursed once every three months. The proportion of the dividend is then divided by four so that it can be paid out over the course of the entire year, one quarter at a time. Every three months constitutes a quarter. Ex-dividend rates are the rates that are announced to be paid out to shareholders as of a particular date. It indicates that shareholders must purchase the shares prior to this date in order to be eligible for dividends. If you buy stock after the date that it goes ex-dividend, then you will be eligible to receive the following dividend, which will be paid out in the next quarter.

Dividends have the potential to be a very lucrative source of income. Together, growing one's wealth through stock appreciation and dividend income makes for a powerful combination. Coco-Cola (KO), which currently has a dividend yield of 3.1%, is the most well-known dividend stock. Coco-Cola is a respected corporation that has a track record of thriving while enduring adverse economic conditions throughout its history. Since the year 1920, the corporation has been distributing dividends to shareholders. That equates to a century! In addition to that, they have maintained a steady rate of dividend growth for the past 59 years! This is an excellent illustration of a dividend stock that has amazing potential.

The distribution of dividends can be compared to the accrual of interest on savings accounts. To become eligible to accumulate interest on your savings, all that is required of you is to put money into your savings account. This is also true for dividends; all that is required of you is to buy the stock and keep it until the date it goes ex-dividend, or to keep buying the stock and doing nothing else to get dividend payments. To be eligible for dividends, it is not necessary to own a position in the company; rather, this possibility is open to each and every shareholder.

The Golden Years

Individuals with a high net worth benefit the most from dividends. That doesn't mean you can't start receiving dividends if you don't have a lot of money, but it does mean that it won't be worth your while to do so. To gain a better understanding, let's take a look at the example:

A Primer On

Individual With a Low Net Worth:

Jeff makes the decision to put all of his ten thousand dollars into shares in Coco-Cola in order to generate a second source of revenue through dividends. When he invests $10,000, he will receive $300 in dividends each year.

Does it appear to be worthwhile?

In the beginning, dividends will simply prevent you from reaching your maximum growth potential. If the only reason you bought the stock was for the dividends, you could put that $10,000 to better use by investing it in something other than the stock market.

Individual With a High Net Worth

Jack makes the decision to put all of his one million dollars into Coco-Cola stock in order to generate a second source of revenue through dividends. With a million dollars, he will receive dividends worth thirty thousand dollars every year.

Isn't this an improved version?

Even though 3% isn't a very high rate of return, $7500 every three months or $2500 every month is still a decent return to take pleasure in.

Tax Benefits Associated with Dividends

The investor is required to pay federal taxes on the dividends in accordance with the tax bracket that they fall into, if the dividends are considered regular income. On the other hand, qualified dividends are subject to taxation based on the capital gains rate. In order to be considered a qualified dividend holder, you must have owned the stock for at least 60 days in the case of common stock and for at least 90 days in the case of preferred stock. Those with lower incomes who receive eligible dividends may be exempt from paying any federal tax at all.

Your Way To Personal Independence

This book is for you if you are a dental professional who is self-employed and who manages a successful practice on your own.

America has always been a location where there is opportunity, independence, and opportunity, not only for residents of America but also for a large number of migrants who understand the value of the possibility to achieve in life. This is true for both American citizens and migrants who come to America.

The concepts of free enterprise and entrepreneurship are inextricably linked. The spirit of working for oneself, starting a business, gaining respect, and being able to exchange that motivation for cash is at the heart of what the American dream is all about.

The challenge that every entrepreneur who has a vision for the future of their industry will eventually encounter is the tendency to get overly preoccupied with one's current salary while simultaneously being unable to formulate a strategy for building one's financial future. The concept of "future bank" refers to the value, total assets, or true abundance that provides the premise for opportunities and choices in one's "retirement years" or later years. True abundance refers to the capital that we put aside to take care of ourselves so that we don't have to worry about trying to create that income.

In the minds of the Freedom Founders, we refer to this future financial plenty as the road that leads to possibility. Your Freedom Number is determined by each of our customers on an individual basis using my limiting Freedom BlueprintTM. The Freedom NumberTM is a monthly income number, as opposed to a collection number (which is what is used by conventional monetary models). This is because typical models use collection numbers. It is the amount of cash that must be available prior to the evaluation in order to provide the "consume rate" or standard of living for our customer.

When a Freedom Number has been established, determining the amount of contributed money that is required to generate the month-to-month income that provides the security a family requires (and needs) becomes a basic mathematical exercise. Investing one's money in capital resources yields a return that is never enough to deplete the initial investment, which, when taken into consideration further, makes it possible to both expand one's financial legacy and make significant philanthropic donations.

 It's an entirely one-of-a-kind model (warning: I'm an adversary, but I'm a very successful adversary), and it can have incredible repercussions for both the hard-working company genius and his family. Comments like "I just wish I had viewed you years ago!" come from people who were involved in the founding of our freedom.

 owing to the fact that an excessive amount of power is delegated to "outside counsels," to whom one must hand up their future financial plans. Why? As a result of the influence of society and Wall Street, even the most intelligent and educated people have been conditioned to believe that managing money and making financial plans are too complicated for the average individual to handle.

My advice to those who have adopted this belief is to simply accept long-term financial assistance from somebody who has already made the life that you aspire to have. This is my advise to people who have adopted this belief. Although we all require the unmistakable legal, tax, and bookkeeping assistance of a legal adviser or CPA, the experience of a home lawyer, or the services of a protection agent, none of these professionals has created the kind of opportunity way of life that you want. Why should you give weight to their advice, regardless of how significant it may be?

After a business owner has put in a lot of effort and seen some success as a result of their efforts, the next step is to formulate a strategy that will lead to safety and inner harmony. While it is true that owning and operating a business paves the path toward realizing a particular way of life, the fact that this is the case does not change the fact that, for the majority of business owners, the exact achievement of which they are proud serves as a barrier that prevents them from enjoying the fruits of their efforts.

After that, there is the option of retiring at that time. The reasonable dental professional has their sights set out on the time when the training can be sold and venture capital prevails, accommodating the spectacular years, and they are doing this by purchasing and conserving.

But in some instances, even the best of us can be derailed by problems. Perhaps you don't make enough money to put into retirement savings; perhaps you started saving for retirement too late; perhaps you lost the majority of your retirement savings during the financial crisis; or perhaps you just don't trust the economy and the government enough to stop working for a steady income.

However, although the vast majority of dental experts have the intention of figuring out how to put their wealth away, not all of them have made the effort to figure out how to increase the value of their investments.

Do you think that describes you? What exactly is your plan in this matter? Do you already have a plan in place? Is everything going as planned with your arrangement?

Do not take yourself too seriously in the event that you try to evade your reply. You are following in the footsteps of some truly remarkable people; a huge number of dental specialists are in a scenario not unlike to yours. The method in which you are reading this book demonstrates that you are either dissatisfied with the status quo or, at the very least, interested in investigating alternative points of view.

There is a better method, as well as a faster approach, to get to the point where opportunities exist and present options. Isn't the essence of an opportunity to have choices?

Continue reading if you want to learn how to secure a bright financial future for yourself and your loved ones in greater detail.

What You Need To Keep An Eye Out For

When selecting passive index funds to invest in, there are a few hazards that investors need to be aware of. The first thing you need to keep an eye out for is managers of exchange-traded funds (ETFs) and index funds arbitrarily switching the benchmark that their funds duplicate. This means that the managers are essentially moving the goalposts and following another index that provides them a higher chance of recruiting investors. This occurs when a fund manager is not producing the desired results for the investment portfolio.

In most cases, new funds from fund companies with a lower reputation engage in this practice. To steer clear of this issue, be sure to invest in funds issued by reputable companies like

Fidelity, Vanguard, and iShares. Each of these fund companies has been in operation for a significant amount of time and currently manages billions of dollars' worth of assets. Their fund managers have been subjected to stringent screening, so you may have peace of mind knowing that your money is in good hands.

Nevertheless, even with these funds, you still need to be on the lookout for when the fund managers switch. Analyze the performance of the fund both before and after the change to ensure that there are not too many significant differences in performance.

Due to the fact that the funds suffer trading fees, the majority of index funds and ETFs will finish behind their respective underlying index. Choose the one that has the best combination of the lowest expense ratio and the least lag in performance. This is the one you should go with. Be careful to give the prospectus of the fund a thorough reading so that you have a solid understanding of the way the manager intends to invest the money.

There isn't much more to say than "we follow this index" in the prospectuses of index funds and passively managed exchange-traded funds (ETFs), therefore the documents are brief. This is good news for people who dislike reading. Maintain a consistent pattern of long-term ownership of these funds while continuing to put money into them on a regular basis.

Although the fundamentals of profitable investment won't be totally applicable in this context, the advice to stick to what you know, build a margin of safety (by adhering to the fundamentals; you can't acquire a fund for less than it's worth), and evaluate management is still relevant. Investing for the long run and minimizing your trading costs by investing once a month or at some other predetermined frequency should be your top priorities when it comes to investing.

Do not be concerned if you are unsure of which exchange-traded funds (ETFs) or index funds to invest in. In the section on the construction of portfolios, I will go over what to purchase. For the time being, it is important to comprehend that indexing is a fantastic passive investment approach that has the potential to earn you money in the long term.

Contradictions in terms

There are a few drawbacks to investing in a manner that is considered passive, the first and most evident of which being the fact that it does not come at no cost. There is no way around the requirement that you pay the manager the annual expense ratio; this obligation is irrevocable. Investing does not cost anything, and you do not need to hire a third party to manage your portfolio if you are ready to put in the time and effort to analyze individual stocks. It is ultimately worth it to pay someone else to handle your portfolio so that you may spend less time doing it and still get the same or better results.

You should also keep in mind that the overall gains you may anticipate earning will be less than what you have the ability to achieve with active management. This is an important consideration to make. The situation is fraught with a multitude of trade-offs. A portfolio that is actively managed has the potential to generate an unlimited amount of money, despite the fact that the likelihood of this occurring is quite low. On the other hand, a fund that is managed passively will generate market average returns, which are far lower than the active fund's prospective returns but are practically likely to be achieved.

This trade-off is not worth it to an aggressive investor who has the time and expertise, which is why I have included it as a negative aspect of the investment opportunity. On the other hand, it will be of tremendous assistance to anybody who lacks the necessary time or knowledge. Buying just one unit of a passive fund allows you to rapidly diversify your portfolio, which is one of the advantages of investing passively rather than actively.

When we get to the section when I talk about constructing a portfolio, I'll devote more time to discussing diversification. For the time being, it is important to recognize that passive investing offers many benefits to individuals who do not wish to accept the risks that are associated with active investment.

The following is a summary of the most important metrics used in stock investing:

1-52 Weeks High-Low: Determine the price of the stock that is now trading in the stock market, and then compare the current price to the high and low prices of the same stock over the course of the past 52 weeks. The idea is simple: stocks with a lower price range in the current market have greater upward potential than stocks that have already attained high 52-week marks. This is because lower price range stocks have more room to grow in value.

2-Market Capitalization: This metric is used to determine how large of a company a particular business is. The market capitalization of a company can be calculated by multiplying the total number of outstanding shares by the current price of those shares on the market. Typically, there are three different classifications of tocks: large cap, mid-cap, and small cap. When compared to some gems that fall under the categories of mid-cap and small-cap companies, large cap stocks like Exxon typically do not have as much potential for an increase in price as do mid-cap and small-cap stocks. The latter category of mid-cap and small-cap companies has the highest possibility of being emerging star investments, which typically multiply and increase by a factor of ten in a given amount of time. These investments are referred to as "emerging star investments."

This metric tells you how many dollars are being traded in a single day and is measured in volume. The amount of volume that is traded in a given day is determined by multiplying the average price by the number of stocks that are traded in that day. The volume of blue chip stocks, such as Exxon, Microsoft, and Apple, is generally higher. Small and mid-cap stocks, on the other hand, have lower volume, which means that there is some risk associated with their liquidity.

4-An increase in earnings (both in the past and in the future): This is an important criterion that is used to establish the value of stock. To get a corporation's earnings per share, or EPS, just divide the total earnings of the company by the total number of outstanding shares. Earnings growth, measured on a year-over-year basis, is significant for two reasons: first, it indicates if earnings have increased over the course of the previous five years; second, it indicates whether actual earnings have exceeded predicted earnings in the current year. The rate of growth of a company's earnings is a particularly useful metric for evaluating the performance of growing companies. The issuance of more shares, or the conversion of fixed income securities into common stocks, both have the effect of diluting earnings per share, which is an interesting phenomenon. The value of EPS would decrease as a result of taking this action. On the other hand, if a company were to buy back its own shares, it would lead to an increase in the earnings per share. in a proportional manner. For instance, if a company with a large cash reserve decides to buy back half of its outstanding shares, the earnings per share (EPS) will mathematically double, making the company more appealing to stock investors. Keep in mind that EPS has a very strong relationship with the price of stock. In the long run, a growth in the price of stocks may be brought about by the repurchase of existing shares under the assumption that no significant changes have been brought about in the relevant external factors.

5-Price to earnings ratio, often known as the P/E ratio: The price-to-earnings ratio is by far the most widely used metric in the world of stock investing, despite the fact that it comes with a few important qualifications. The price-to-earnings ratio, or P/E ratio, is calculated by dividing the current stock price by the company's earnings from the previous 12 months (although analysts will also often use earnings forecasted for the next 12 months). Regardless of which way the stock price moves, growth investors want to see an increase in earnings for the company they own. On the other hand, value investors are looking for a falling price-to-earnings ratio so that they might find bargains among the available options. In general, value investors look for businesses that have a better profits growth rate than the P/E ratio at the time of the investment. The fact that the current price-to-earnings ratio is lower than the average for the previous five years is the second metric that the value investor looks for in a good investment.

6-The Ratio of Price to Sales, or P/S: It is a commonly held belief that certain businesses will adjust their accounting procedures in order to artificially inflate their profits. To apply any kind of alteration to the ale statistics would be a fairly difficult task. The amount of money that you are willing to pay for the sales that are generated by the company can be determined with the help of this metric. This number should continue to decrease for companies that are experiencing growth. On the other hand, growth investors won't be too concerned about this ratio, especially when compared to value investors. A value investor's ideal scenario is one in which this ratio is lower.

7-Price to Book ratio (sometimes written as P/B): The book value of a company indicates how much it would be worth if it were liquidated at the current time. A simple comparison of the price of the stock to the net asset value of the company is represented by the price to book ratio. The most important thing to keep in mind is that this metric places an emphasis on the actual assets of the company. The results of certain study on investments indicate that intangible assets also play a very significant part in the process of creating value for shareholders. This is one of the reasons why the price-to-book ratio is not an all-encompassing metric.

Metrics for the creation and growth of value, number eight: The earnings per share (EPS) metric has traditionally been the primary area of focus for most stock analysts during the past five years. It is possible to make a mistake if you base your stock investment decision solely on a company's earnings or its sale, despite the fact that earnings and sale are similar to a company's life bloodline. More specifically, the analyst needs to do a more in-depth analysis of the following three key areas, all of which contribute to the eventual earnings (ale) of the company:

a. The quality of the revenue that the company actually brings in and the transparency (compliance standard) of how revenue is recognized. What are the opportunities for expansion that the company has?

b. The percentage of net profits made or the level of earnings: What kind of approach does a business take to maximize their return on investment while minimizing their costs? Naturally, good management plays a significant role in increasing both the quantity and quality of earnings.

c: What is the current status of the cash flow? It is essential to make investments in publicly traded companies that have positive cash flows.

This metric is generally useful for large blue chip companies, such as those that make up the Dow Jones Industrial Average. The 9-Dividend Yield is an example of one such metric. It is more significant for "small and high growth companies" because those companies almost never declare dividends, thus that's why it's more relevant. Some investors, depending on their risk tolerance and the objectives they have for their investments, will favor large companies that consistently generate dividends.

10-Relative Price Strength: This metric analyzes the price performance of "tock" within a similar group over the course of the previous year. A comparison between tick and sibling was also made for earnings per hare. Typically, Investor's Business Daily is the organization that conducts analyses of this kind.

11-Return on Equity (ROE): This is a very essential indicator that explains how much money the company is making off of the equity that its shareholders have invested in the business. It clarifies if the organization is producing a profit, effectively employing the resources it has available, and using those resources in an efficient manner. This indicator is especially important for growth investors to take into consideration. Return on Equity (ROE) is an important metric for companies undergoing rapid expansion to monitor in order to ensure that their growth initiatives are producing a positive net present value (NPV). The Return on Equity (ROE) metric provides a clear indication of the breadth and expertise of the management.

12-Insider Ownership: It is often thought that the larger size of the insider ownership is a stronger indicator of the success of a company. This is because insider ownership tends to be passed down from generation to generation. This proposition makes sense because if the owners also had a share in the company, they would be more motivated to work hard to ensure its continued success. Nevertheless, this metric by itself is not sufficient to determine the strength of a company. It is possible that there will be times when shareholders decide to sell their equities in order to generate money to satisfy their shifting personal and professional needs.

13-Projections on the future performance of the Company: The value of a company is not determined by its performance in the past. This is due to the fact that past performance is only meaningful to the extent that it can assist analysts in coming up with certain predictions regarding future trends and growth. On the other hand, there is no assurance that the company will be able to achieve the same level of success as in the past or that the external environment will remain the same. The projection (prediction) of the company's future earnings and revenue is a task that is exceptionally challenging. Investors are responsible for conducting their own research as part of their due diligence in order to evaluate the likelihood of achieving the targeted levels of real earnings and revenue.

14-The Integrity of Management and the Depth of It: This metric is possibly the most important one to consider when making an assessment regarding the potential performance and course of any company in the future. Performance is a relative concept, and it will change based on the kind of business being discussed. For instance, when viewed from the perspective of growing companies, performance is characterized by year-over-year (YOY) growth that is sustained by a good return on equity (ROE). The performance of a technology company is dependent on the successful launch of innovation cloaked in the guise of new product introduction. One important disclaimer to keep in mind is that innovation is notoriously difficult to quantify because it encompasses both the concrete and the ethereal realms. How, for instance, can one evaluate the success of, or the worth over the long term of, Apple's iPhones? This effort is made even more difficult by the widespread availability of disruptive technologies. The breadth, maturity, and devotion of a company's management team is the single most important factor in determining how well a business will perform in the future.

15-The Stock Market's Volatility: This metric is of the utmost importance in the process of arriving at decisions regarding the risk-reward profile of the investor. Simply said, volatility is a measurement of how much the returns on an investment deviate from the average value over a specified amount of time. A higher level of volatility indicates a higher level of risk. In the short run, volatility is more likely to be elevated, however in the long run, it is more likely to become more stable. Volatility is, of course, dependent on the correlation of stock price fluctuations to market movements, which is referred to as a beta.

In order to reach a conclusion, a holistic approach to analysis of the aforementioned framework is required. Again, the value and growth investor will have a different perspective on the metric when it has been coupled with the other metrics. The value investor's primary concerns would be the company's long-term competitive advantage, the reputation of the brand,

and the relative value of the company at the present time. On the other hand, growth investors are more concerned with a company's historical and projected rates of growth, regardless of the 52-week price changes and the growth potential (revenue generation) of the company.

Money That Can Be Programmed

This is not the currency that was around when your grandparents were young. To put it another way, it's not the money that your parents have saved up. This is cash that can be totally programmed and scripted, and its skills can be fine-tuned to a high degree of specificity. You have the ability to decide who can access it, when they can do so, and how it can potentially be dispersed. A completely new field known as "smart contracts" has emerged, and it now enables us to program the behavior of entire systems that can also manage money.

The word "cash" is a particularly inadequate choice to employ in this context due to the fact that we frequently deal with objects that may give the impression of being currency but are not, in fact, cash. What are some things that can be said regarding loyalty points, tokens, metro cards, and air mile accumulation? What are some things that may be made about the statement of someone being a fan of Justin Bieber and being granted full access to the music index as a token? What can be claimed regarding the numerous brands that are capable of being converted into tokens and created into a worldwide replaceable framework by utilizing this protocol directly on the internet?

On January 3, 2009, the globe underwent significant shift. Since that time, more than a thousand more cryptocurrencies have been formed following the same process, and almost all of them include open-source code. They are expanding in every direction, researching every imaginable niche of this environment, every minute difference in capacities and elements, creating new business sectors, and generating capital for a large number of new enterprises all over the world. A significant number of software developers and designers are getting ready to take advantage of this new invention. The web as we know it is undergoing tremendous development.

These days, there are self-employed professionals who are making use of money on the internet; generally speaking, they are not subject to the regulation of any particular state.

1.2.4 Blockchains Hosted on the Intranet

What plans do the world's largest corporations have for the brand-new network that is mystical, open, decentralized, impartial, borderless, and safe from restrictions?

They are going to remark, "Wow! That sounds good to us... However, would you be able to remove the open, decentralized, independent, borderless, and restriction-safe qualities and bundle them with a support level agreement (SLA), a yearly permit, and control? Control for the both of us. They are going to replicate the World Wide Web on their internal networks. They will create closed nurseries of monotonous, flat material that is typically unstable and sits on the patio of businesses offering a little bit of substantial value. It will be shielded from the onslaught of technological progress that is occurring all around us because it will exist outside of the cooperation of the global local area.

They will establish intranets, they will promise victory, they will change course, and at the end of it all, they will say, "We created Blockchain." They will be off-base, and their attempt will be unsuccessful.

1.2.5 Consensus Achieved Through Distribution

There isn't even a blockchain involved in this inNovation, and that's not even the most exciting part. A data set relic that was created out of this convention is called a blockchain. No, the real excitement stems from the fact that it is possible to reach a mediated agreement between parties that do not trust one another, across vast distances, with virtually no central party, authority, or intermediary. This ability has sparked a lot of interest in the cryptocurrency space.

From the outside looking in, the agreement appears to be chaotic, muddled, and weird. The internet is something that absolutely everyone in this room is aware of, and it is something that is open, equal, weird, and not understood by partnerships. We have done it in the past, and we are going to do it again. When we do this again, we shall bring the entire globe with us.

A Breakdown Of How The Covered Call Operates

One of these three approaches is how covered calls are completed.
The price of the stock continues to fall. In this scenario, the value of the covered call will be zero when it comes time for it to expire. The bad news is that the stock price will go down, but the good news is that the seller will get to keep the premium, and they will thus still earn money from the deal. Owning shares in a company entails the inherent risk of experiencing price fluctuations, such as the recent drop in the stock's value. You ought to have taken this into consideration before you completed the purchase. Keep in mind that you need to

be willing to hold that stock regardless of what happens, so make an informed decision. It is important to keep in mind, however, that the profit made from selling the call can help to compensate for the fall in the price of the stock.

There is a possibility that the share price will drop before the contract's end date. You do not need to be concerned about being stuck in this posture for an infinite amount of time as a result of this fact. Even though the stock price has decreased and the call value has decreased as well, you still have the opportunity to buy the call back for a price that is lower than the price at which you sold it.

There is either no change in the stock price or a very slight increase.

This is not a situation in which one would lose. Even though the covered call will become worthless when it expires, the premium that was paid for the option will still be kept by the seller. Even if the price increase is only minimal, the seller will still benefit from it if there is even a little increase in the price of the stock. This is because the holder of the option will probably not exercise their right to gain from the price increase.

When the Stock Price Is Greater Than the Strike Price

The holder of the option will exercise their right to buy the stock if the share price rises over the strike price before the option's expiration date. In this scenario, the seller will be required to sell the 100 shares of stock. Even if you had already made peace with the reality that you would be willing to part with the stock before the price of the stock skyrockets, it is still a bitter pill to swallow. However, you may console yourself with the knowledge that you will make the most profit possible from the transaction.

The Money Lender's Perspective on Borrowing and Lending

Lenders are able to provide people money because they make careful, calculated decisions depending on the amount of risk involved. They hope, first and foremost, that they will be repaid, and second, that they will make a profit from the transaction. Lenders will look at both your current and your previous financial situations to determine whether or not you are able to meet the two criteria that they have set forth for receiving financing.

When evaluating your credit history, financial institutions will take into consideration the following factors:

1. The history of your credit. They will look at the total amount and number of loans that have been repaid in the past, as well as the size and quantity of loans

that have been repaid. In addition to that, they will look at your FICO ratings in addition to other info that is fundamental.

2. A record of previous earnings. How have your previous investments performed in terms of profits? what is the track record of your other investments?

How much longer is it going to take? They will review your income statements and tax returns for the past three years, as well as your debt and any court judgements that may have an impact on your current financial condition. In addition, they will look at any past legal decisions that may have an impact on your current financial situation.

3. Any prior experience you have had with loans. The essence of the question that the lender seeks to answer is whether or not they can rely on you to

uphold your end of the loan agreement. This indicates that you need to be reliable and make solid decisions on commercial matters.

4. present state of one's finances and material possessions Lenders are especially concerned with your liquidity, which comprises your revenue and cash flow.

Lenders will want to know about all of your property expenditures when determining whether or not you have the ability to create a profit from your business. How much does it cost you to maintain the property so that it stays in good condition? What will the rates be for your insurance, how much will the taxes be, and how much will the repairs cost? The lender will want to make sure that you are able to pay their interest rates in addition to the expenditures associated with property ownership. Although lengthier payback durations are often more beneficial to the consumer, shorter payback intervals are frequently preferred by lenders. When you choose a payback period that is longer, you are able to save origination fees, additional appraisal fees, and other costs. When it comes to loans for investment property, a loan with a fixed interest rate for 20 years is regarded to have a long term. A balloon payment is one that is made on a loan between the fifth and tenth year of its term.

In the event that your lender makes an effort to coerce you into agreeing to a shorter payback period, you may devise a strategy in which you re-price the loan every five years as an alternative to having to pay a significant amount of money all at once. A common choice is to take the existing prime interest rate and add one percentage point to it.

Keep in mind that the majority of the terms associated with real estate investment can be negotiated, and that your lender could potentially be a partner in real estate investment. You are only going to come out ahead if you put in the effort to cultivate a solid, long-term working relationship with your lender.

The Diversify Method, Chapter 7

Having investments in a variety of different areas is essential to ensure your financial security. The first chapter began with an illustration of how one could use a 529 savings account to make preparations for their child's future schooling. Although this kind of account is quite useful, and many families will be able to save enough money to cover the cost of their child's education, it does not serve any other function besides that of education. The investments you make need to be catered to your specific requirements in order to be successful. Only a single component of what you require from your future finances can be satisfied by the 529 plan. In addition, you will need to make preparations for retirement, establish an emergency fund, and accumulate additional investment capital that you can use for further high-risk ventures. The most important thing to keep in mind while diversifying your holdings is to ensure that all of your financial obligations are satisfied and not to rely on high-risk assets to pay for essential expenses.

The 529 college plan is a terrific investment, but I would hardly claim that the interest earned or even the lower tax penalty on withdraws is its greatest value. The 529 college plan is a great investment. The most important benefit of the 529 plan is that it motivates people to save money on a regular basis for a sufficient amount of time so that their children will have a sufficient amount of money for education when they reach the age of eligibility for college. The 529 plan is the only investment opportunity that comes close to fitting the current circumstances quite as well as it does, but there are plenty of other investments that have the possibility of yielding larger interest.

Aware of the Dangers

When you invest your money in various accounts, you need to be aware of which accounts are secure investments and which accounts are more risky so that you can make the appropriate allocations. Every investment carries with it the possibility of experiencing a loss, but some losses are just less likely to occur than others. If U.S. Treasury bonds were to lose all of their value, the money that is backed up by those bonds would not be nearly as significant as the larger national crisis that would have to be occurring at the time. On the other hand, you could make plans to save up for college by putting away a little bit of money each month in a savings account, and then you could use that money to invest in the stock market or the foreign exchange market. Although this form of high-risk investment might help you reach your objective of having enough money saved for education, the risk involved is simply too enormous. The same is true when it comes to setting money aside for your retirement or your home mortgage. There are certain investments that must be protected at all costs, while others can withstand a greater degree of uncertainty. You need to make sure that the risks you incur are commensurate with the dangers you are willing to accept for however you want to use the money you invest in other things.

The Most Efficient Distribution of Resources

Knowing the risks associated with each of your investments is necessary in order to determine the most effective distribution of your wealth. Every circumstance will be unique, and the manner in which you choose to allocate your resources will be determined by a wide range of factors that I have no way of determining in advance. The most reliable method for determining whether or not you are effectively distributing your resources is to evaluate each investment in light of the function that it is intended to perform. Some investment portfolios are going to have an overall level of risk that is significantly higher than other investment portfolios. It's not about how good you are at investing or even how much money you make; this has a lot more to do with how you live your life. A man who is childless, unmarried, and living on his own will require much less security in his investments than a married parent with three kids. Because he does not have to provide for other people in his home, the man who lives alone can take a greater risk with his other assets. However, he will still need to have safe investments like a 401(k). In this situation, the single man should have a different investment for each of his financial goals; nevertheless, each of his goals is significantly less essential than the goals of the married father. A fund that is used for extra vacations or for planning a family might be created using investment money that is set aside for use after retirement. Both of these objectives are vital, but one of them should take precedence over the other when considering investment opportunities.

As you progress through life, you should anticipate that your investing strategy will require ongoing adjustments. Your income and the cost of living are both going to fluctuate, and so will your savings goals. The best method to diversify your portfolio is to make adjustments to this investing strategy so that it takes into account your objectives. You do not have to break apart your portfolio only for the purpose of diversification; as long as each of your financial goals is protected and assumes the level of risk that you are prepared to take, you will have a diverse portfolio that is suitable for your requirements without making any additional investments.

Methods That Have Proven Successful In Determining The Stock's Intrinsic Value

1. Diverse sources of financial gain

It is one of the most common approaches that people take when determining the value of a stock. Having said that, it's not completely accurate either. With this approach, you may choose any valuation number of the firm that was provided in the most current report and then compare it to the value of the company.

The net income, EBIT (Earnings Before Interest and Taxes), and EBITDA (Earnings Before Interest, Taxes, Depreciation, and Amortization), among other financial metrics, are frequently relied upon by investors. Do you remember when we talked about the P/E ratio? To put it another way, it's the same as basing the value of the company on its net income. Instead of relying solely on the P/E ratio, it is commonly advised that enterprise value be compared to EBIDTA or EBIT instead. Value of the enterprise is market capitalization plus market debt minus cash and equivalents.

2. A CASH FLOW WITH DISCOUNTS

It is imperative that you make use of this strategy whenever you are searching for opportunities to invest in businesses that maintain sizable cash reserves. The majority of these are considered to be blue-chip firms. Learning this strategy is important because it allows you to estimate the cash flow of the firm as well as your personal potential for becoming a majority or full owner of the business in the future.

To calculate the current value of the stock, all you need to do is follow a straightforward formula. To put it another way, if you expect to earn a cash flow of one hundred dollars every year for the next ten years, should you pay one thousand dollars for that number of shares? Not at all, of course! There are a few other factors, such as inflation, that will diminish the quantity of money over time, and your $1,000 won't be worth nearly as much in ten years as it is today. You may even find out the future cash flow of a company using this, and then adjust your bid accordingly. After you have that value, all you have to do is compare it to the current value of the share, and you will have determined the stock's intrinsic worth, as well as whether or not it is now over- or under-valued. The fact that you will be dealing with assumptions and predictions of the data is the one and only drawback to using this strategy. As a consequence of this, there is opportunity for error. Either it will work marvelously for you or it will not work at all for you; either way, it is an essential instrument for you to have in your armory.

3. The formula developed by Benjamin Graham

In the previous chapters, we may have only skimmed the surface of this particular topic, but in this one, we will go much farther into depth. This technique is useful for cyclical businesses that sell popular things when the economy is doing well since it helps them maximize their profits. It encompasses a variety of things such as hotel chains and airfares. However, it can also be employed for businesses that have a cash flow that is unpredictable or for businesses that are very new and do not have much of a history.

We are all aware that Benjamin was a value investor who was constantly on the lookout for opportunities to purchase a collection of powerful stocks at a price that was more affordable.

His brilliant book, "The intelligent investor," in which he proposed a formula to determine the intrinsic value of a stock, was afterwards amended by him. The formula was initially introduced by him. V represents the intrinsic value, EPS stands for earnings per share, g denotes the rate of growth over the previous decade or two, and Y indicates the current rate of return. The procedure is as follows:

V is EPS (8.5 x 2g) multiplied by 4.4/Y.

Since this formula was first published in 1962, it is possible that it may not reflect the world as it is today in every way. There are a number of people who have made various changes to this formula in order to make it more precise. In any event, the essential nature of the thing is unaltered.

4. THE ULTIMATE SPORTS EXERCISE FORMULA

I strongly suggest that you utilize this reliable approach to the valuation of stocks for any kind of business. This formula raises the company's PE value in a manner that is proportional to the company's basic values, which include earning growth rate, dividend yield, business risk, financial risk, and earning visibility.

If a firm's fundamentals are solid, the PE will rise, which will result in an increase in the company's value. On the other hand, if the fundamentals of a company are unstable, this will result in a decrease in the company's value. Basically, you will give a value to each of the factors that have been discussed above, and then you will determine the PE by applying the formula that is presented here:

Reasonable Price PE equals the basic PE [1 + (1 - Business Risk)] is equal to X. X equals "1 plus (1 minus Financial Risk)" X equals "1 plus (1 minus Earnings Visibility)"

5. THE CURRENT NET-NET VALUE OF THE ASSETS

If you want to determine whether or not the stock price of the company is reasonable in relation to its net assets, you have no choice but to utilize this formula. It is not going to work for a corporation with little assets. You will do a comprehensive analysis of the balance sheet and obtain an estimate of the value of the tangible assets. Software-based businesses do not fit into the parameters of this approach at all. Because it provides a reference to the fundamental worth of a stock, knowing the liquidation value of the company is one of the most important things you can do. When their stock price is lower than the base or floor value, the companies are eligible to be classified as net-nets.

The worth of a company's net current assets is easy to calculate. Simply deduct all of the obligations from the present asset, and you will have your answer. People have lost their minds if they buy a stock that has a negative earnings yield, unless the company in question either doesn't have a good business plan or is wasting money at an alarming rate.

6. THE REPRODUCTIVE VALUE OF THE ASSET

If you want to know what it would take for a competitor to replicate the original firm, having this model is absolutely necessary. You will gain an understanding of the genuine costs involved in constructing a copy of an existing business at this stage. It is a lengthy model that takes several inputs from your end; in addition, it requires that you assess each line in the balance sheet and determine the adjustment, if any, that is required. In the end, the value that you estimate will serve as the basis for determining the true value of the existing company that you are interested in investing in.

7. Earnings Power Value (EPV), abbreviated as "EPV"

You will be able to locate several worthwhile prospective businesses by using this strategy. As I indicated up top, you can think of this strategy as an extension of the asset reproductive value.

The algorithm in and of itself is quite easy to understand; however, determining the profits amount is a little bit complicated. To accomplish this, you will need to review the income statement of the company in order to identify any necessary corrections. The expected present value (EPV) is anticipated to skyrocket with an improved competitive edge. It is quite difficult to estimate the actual growth of a firm because there are a variety of things affecting it that have never been seen before; as a result, you will most likely be fine if you continue to use the EPV for the time being.

www.ingramcontent.com/pod-product-compliance
Lightning Source LLC
Chambersburg PA
CBHW011842200326
41597CB00026B/4679